I am a Great White Shark

أنا القرش الأبيض الكبير

Karen Durrie

كارين دوري

ARABIC/ENGLISH BILINGUAL
AV²
BY WEIGL™
ADDED VALUE • AUDIO VISUAL

Go to www.av2books.com, and enter this book's unique code.

BOOK CODE

M809304

AV² by Weigl brings you media enhanced books that support active learning.

AV² provides enriched content that supplements and complements this book. Weigl's AV² books strive to create inspired learning and engage young minds in a total learning experience.

Your AV² Media Enhanced book comes alive with...

The AV² Arabic language collection gives emerging bilingual readers access to both a printed Arabic and English book and a bilingual eBook that provides Arabic and English translations of the text.

Simply log on to www.av2books.com and enter the book code found on page 2 of this book to unlock the bilingual eBook. Readers can then use the on-screen navigation buttons to flip through the pages of the online eBook. Both the printed book and online eBook display English and Arabic text on the same page to help readers learn Arabic and English vocabulary and sentence structure.

I can drink 227 bottles of water in 10 minutes.
بإمكاني شرب 227 زجاجة ماء في 10 دقائق.

Published by AV² by Weigl
350 5th Avenue, 59th Floor New York, NY 10118
Website: www.av2books.com   www.weigl.com

ISBN: 978-1-61913-884-1 (hardcover)

Printed in the United States of America in North Mankato, Minnesota
1 2 3 4 5 6 7 8 9 0 16 15 14 13 12

092012
WEP240912

Project Coordinator: Aaron Carr
Art Director: Terry Paulhus
Translator: Maei Jeneidi

Weigl acknowledges Getty Images as the primary image supplier for this title.

I am a Great White Shark

In this book, I will teach you about

- myself
- my food
- my home
- my family

and much more!

أنا القرش الأبيض الكبير

في هذا الكتاب سوف أعلّمكم عن

نفسي

طعامي

بيتي

عائلتي

و الكثير غير ذلك!

I am a great white shark.

أنا القرش الأبيض الكبير.

4

I am the biggest fish
in the ocean
that hunts its food.

أنا أكبر سمكة في المحيط

تصطاد طعامها.

7

I have skin that feels like sand paper.

لي جلد ملمسه مثل ملمس

ورق الصنفرة.

9

I do not have any bones
in my body.

لا يوجد أي عظام في جسمي.

11

I can smell
one drop of blood
from three miles away.

أستطيع أن أشم رائحة قطرة دماء

واحدة عن بعد ثلاثة أميال.

I can swim
when I am asleep.

بإمكاني السباحة و أنا نائم.

I grow new teeth all my life.

تنمو لي أسنان جديدة طوال حياتي.

I can find a heart beat from 9 feet away.

بإمكاني أن أشعر بقلب ينبض عن بعد 9 أقدام.

19

I have a big fin on my back.

لدي زعنفة كبيرة على ظهري.

I am a great white shark.

أنا القرش الأبيض الكبير.

SHARK FACTS

These pages provide detailed information that expands on the interesting facts found in the book. They are intended to be used by adults as a learning support to help young readers round out their knowledge of each amazing animal featured in the I Am series.

معلومات عن القرش الأبيض الكبير

توفر هذه الصفحة المزيد من التفاصيل حول الحقائق المثيرة الموجودة في هذا الكتاب. وضعت هذه الحقائق لكي يستخدمها الكبار كوسيلة لدعم تعليم القراء الصغار و الإضافة إلى معرفتهم بكل حيوان يتم استعراضه في سلسلة «أنا».

Pages 4–5

الصفحة ٤ - ٥

I am a great white shark. Great white sharks live in coastal waters in oceans all over the world. When they are born, they are called pups. They swim away from their mother right away and look after themselves. Great white shark pups are about 5 feet (1.5 meters) long.

أنا القرش الأبيض الكبير. تعيش أسماك القرش الأبيض الكبير في المياه الساحلية من المحيطات في جميع أنحاء العالم. عند ولادتها، يطلق عليها اسم «فراخ». تسبح الفراخ بعيدا عند أمها بعد الولادة مباشرة و تقوم بالإعتناء بنفسها. يصل طول فراخ سمك القرش الأبيض إلى ما يعادل 5 أقدام (1.5 متر).

Pages 6–7

الصفحة ٦ - ٧

Great white sharks are the biggest fish in the ocean that hunt food. Great white sharks are the biggest predatory fish on Earth. They can reach more than 20 feet (6 m) long, and can grow to more than 5,000 pounds (2,268 kilograms). This is as heavy as a pickup truck.

أسماك القرش الأبيض الكبير هي الأكبر في المحيط التي تصطاد طعامها. تعد أسماك القرش الابيض الكبير هي أكبر الأسماك المفترسة على الأرض. يمكن أن يصل طولها إلى أكثر من 20 قدم (6 أمتار)، ويمكن أن ينمو حجمها إلى أكثر من 5,000 رطل (2,268 كيلوغرام)، أي ما يعادل وزن شاحنة نقل صغيرة.

Pages 8–9

الصفحة ٨ - ٩

Great white sharks have skin that feels like sand paper. The great white shark's skin is covered with a layer of tiny teeth called denticles. These denticles make the shark's skin feel rough, like sandpaper, in one direction, but if touched in the other direction, the skin feels smooth.

لأسماك القرش الأبيض الكبير جلد ملمسه مثل ملمس ورق الصنفرة. تغطي جسم القرش الابيض الكبير طبقة أسنان صغيرة جدا يطلق عليها اسم «الشّغرين». تجعل هذه الطبقة جلد سمكة القرش خشن الملمس مثل ورق الصنفرة عند لمسه في اتجاه واحد، ولكن إذا لمست في الاتجاه الآخر تكون ملساء.

Great white sharks do not have any bones in their bodies. A shark's skeleton is made of cartilage. This is the same as the bendy material that makes up the flexible part of people's ears and noses. Cartilage helps sharks to turn quickly when they swim.

لا يوجد أي عظام في جسم القرش الأبيض الكبير. إن تكوين الهيكل العظمي للقرش الأبيض الكبير هو عبارة عن غضروف. مثله مثل المادة المرنة الموجودة في آذان و أنوف الناس. وجود هذا الغضروف يساعد القرش الأبيض الكبير على الإلتفاف بسرعة عند السباحة.

Pages 10–11

الصفحة ١٠ - ١١

Great white sharks can smell one drop of blood from 3 miles (4.8 kilometers) away. Sharks can also sense one drop of blood in a billion drops of water. They have large nostrils on their nose. Their nostrils are not used for breathing, just for smelling.

باستطاعة أسماك القرش الأبيض الكبير أن تشم رائحة قطرة دماء واحدة عن بعد ثلاثة أميال (4.8 كلم). بإمكان سمك القرش الإحساس بوجود قطرة دماء واحدة بين الملايين من قطرات الماء. لسمك القرش منخرين كبيرين على أنفه يستخدمهما للشم فقط و لا للتنفس.

Pages 12–13

الصفحة ١٢ - ١٣

Great white sharks swim when they sleep. Sharks need to keep moving so that water flows over their gills. This keeps oxygen flowing through them. Sharks do not close their eyes when they sleep. They rest one side of their brain at a time in order to get their sleep.

بإمكان أسماك القرش الأبيض الكبير السباحة و هي نائمة. تحتاج أسماك القرش إلى التحرك بشكل مستمر لكي يتدفق الماء على خياشيمها، الشئ الذي يبقي الأكسجين متدفقا فيها. كما أنها لا تغمض أعينها عندما تنام، فهي تريح جانبا واحدا من دماغها بالتناوب لتتمكن من النوم.

Pages 14–15

الصفحة ١٤ - ١٥

Great white sharks grow new teeth all their life. Great white sharks have about 300 sharp, triangular teeth in several rows in their mouths. Their teeth fall out easily and often, and they grow new ones to replace them.

تنمو لأسماك القرش الأبيض الكبير أسنان جديدة طوال حياتها. لأسماك القرش الأبيض الكبير عدة صفوف من الأسنان الحادة مثلثة الشكل في فمها و التي تقدر بـ 300 سن. من الغالب و السهل سقوط أسنان القرش لذا ينمو لها أسنان جديدة لإستبدال التي سقطت.

Pages 16–17

الصفحة ١٦ - ١٧

Great white sharks can find a heartbeat from 9 feet (2.7 m) away. Sharks have tiny holes in their snouts. These holes lead to canals in their heads that are filled with a kind of jelly. The jelly helps sharks sense electrical currents, including the heartbeats and muscle movements of people and animals.

بإمكان أسماك القرش الأبيض الكبير أن تشعر بقلب ينبض عن بعد 9 أقدام (2.7 متر). لسمك القرش ثقوب صغيرة جدا على خطمه. تؤدي هذه الثقوب إلى قنوات في رأسه مملوءة بنوع من الهلام. يساعد الهلام أسماك القرش على استشعار التيارات الكهربائية، بما في ذلك نبضات قلب وحركات عضلات الناس والحيوانات.

Pages **الصفحة**
18–19 **١٨ - ١٩**

Great white sharks have big fins on their backs. Great white sharks are a vulnerable species. They can get caught in fishing nets and are often killed for their body parts. In some parts of the world, shark fins are used to make soup. There are fewer than 3,500 great white sharks left in the world.

لأسماك القرش الأبيض الكبير زعنفة كبيرة على ظهرها. إن أسماك القرش الأبيض الكبير هي فصائل معرضة للخطر. من الممكن اصطيادها بشباك الصيد حيث تقتل غالبا للحصول على أعضاء جسمها. في بعض أجزاء العالم تستخدم زعانف سمك القرش في صنع الحساء. هناك أقل من 3,500 سمكة قرش ابيض كبير متبقية في العالم.

Pages **الصفحة**
20–21 **٢٠ - ٢١**

ARABIC/ENGLISH BILINGUAL
AV2 BY WEIGL™
ADDED VALUE • AUDIO VISUAL

Check out www.av2books.com to access the bilingual eBook in Arabic and English.

1 Go to av2books.com

2 Enter book code [M 8 0 9 3 0 4]

3 Explore your shark book!

www.av2books.com